Go to **www.ketoveo.com** for more guides and resources to help you on your keto journey.

Contents

28 Day

Meal Planning

Welcome to the Ketoveo tribe for your meal planning over the next 28 days. Here you can follow our step-by-step ready-made recipes over the next four weeks. You can also follow your very own creative meal planning ideas with the use of the Ketoveo shopping list and friendly food list to see what meal plans you want to create over the next 28 days.

Let's get you started on your journey into ketosis!

Here are our suggested meal plans, including all recipes, for your next 28 days. Feel free to mix them up however you wish and simply have fun with it!

Week One:

Day 1	Day 2	Day 3	Day 4
Breakfast	**Breakfast**	**Breakfast**	**Breakfast**
Spinach, Feta Scrambled Eggs	Almond Cocoa Protein Smoothie	Spinach, Feta Scrambled Eggs	Coconut/Almond Pancakes
Lunch	**Lunch**	**Lunch**	**Lunch**
Bacon, Avocado & Egg Salad	Sliced Steak with Brussels Sprouts	Lettuce Hamburger Beef Patty	Zesty Shrimp & Avocado Salad
Dinner	**Dinner**	**Dinner**	**Dinner**
Garlic Chicken with Broccoli & Spinach	Grilled Salmon with Avocado Salsa	Chicken Taco Lettuce Wraps	Garlic Chicken with Broccoli & Spinach

Day 5	Day 6	Day 7
Breakfast	**Breakfast**	**Breakfast**
Omelet with Onions, Peppers & Cheese	Almond Cocoa Protein Smoothie	Omelet with Onions, Peppers & Cheese
Lunch	**Lunch**	**Lunch**
Bacon, Avocado & Egg Salad	Lettuce Hamburger Beef Patty	Zesty Shrimp & Avocado Salad
Dinner	**Dinner**	**Dinner**
Grilled Salmon with Avocado Salsa	Garlic Shrimp Zucchini Pasta	Chicken Taco Lettuce Wraps

Week Two:

Day 8	Day 9	Day 10	Day 11
Breakfast	**Breakfast**	**Breakfast**	**Breakfast**
Coconut/Almond Pancakes	Omelet with Onions, Peppers & Cheese	Avocado Mint Green Smoothie	Yogurt, Almond Butter Raspberries & Coconut
Lunch	**Lunch**	**Lunch**	**Lunch**
Lettuce Hamburger Beef Patty	Zesty Shrimp & Avocado Salad	Chicken Wings, Celery Sticks & Nut Dip	Chops Marinated in Red Pesto
Dinner	**Dinner**	**Dinner**	**Dinner**
Garlic Shrimp Zucchini Pasta	Chicken Taco Lettuce Wraps	Garlic Steak Bites	Sesame Salmon with Baby Bok Choy & Mushrooms

Day 12	Day 13	Day 14	
Breakfast	**Breakfast**	**Breakfast**	
Avocado Mint Green Smoothie	Yogurt, Almond Butter Raspberries & Coconut	Avocado Mint Green Smoothie	
Lunch	**Lunch**	**Lunch**	
Lettuce Hamburger Beef Patty	Chicken Wings, Celery Sticks & Nut Dip	Chops Marinated in Red Pesto	
Dinner	**Dinner**	**Dinner**	
Pesto Chicken & Veggies	Sesame Salmon with Baby Bok Choy & Mushrooms	Garlic Steak Bites	

Week Three:

Day 15	Day 16	Day 17	Day 18
Breakfast	**Breakfast**	**Breakfast**	**Breakfast**
Almond Cocoa Protein Smoothie	Boiled Eggs & Avocado	Yogurt, Almond Butter Raspberries & Coconut	Coconut Almond Hot Cereal
Lunch	**Lunch**	**Lunch**	**Lunch**
Avocado Tuna Salad	Chops Marinated in Red Pesto	Zesty Shrimp & Avocado Salad	Avocado Tuna Salad
Dinner	**Dinner**	**Dinner**	**Dinner**
Sesame Salmon with Baby Bok Choy & Mushrooms	Pesto Chicken & Veggies	Stir-Fry Chicken & Veggies	Thai Coconut Soup

Day 19	Day 20	Day 21
Breakfast	**Breakfast**	**Breakfast**
Almond Cocoa Protein Smoothie	Boiled Eggs & Avocado	Coconut Almond Hot Cereal
Lunch	**Lunch**	**Lunch**
Chops Marinated in Red Pesto	Zesty Shrimp & Avocado Salad	Caesar Salad
Dinner	**Dinner**	**Dinner**
Lemon Garlic Steak	Stir-Fry Chicken & Veggies	Garlic Shrimp Zucchini Pasta

Week Four:

Day 22	Day 23	Day 24	Day 25
Breakfast	**Breakfast**	**Breakfast**	**Breakfast**
Fried Eggs & Crispy Bacon	Almond Cocoa Protein Smoothie	Fried Eggs with Avocado	Avocado Mint Green Smoothie
Lunch	**Lunch**	**Lunch**	**Lunch**
Garlic Chicken Zoodles	Chops Marinated in Red Pesto	Garlic Chicken Zoodles	Salmon & Broccoli Saute
Dinner	**Dinner**	**Dinner**	**Dinner**
Garlic Steak Bites	Stir-Fry Chicken & Veggies	Garlic Shrimp Zucchini Pasta	Pesto Chicken & Veggies

Day 26	Day 27	Day 28	
Breakfast	**Breakfast**	**Breakfast**	
Fried Eggs & Crispy Bacon	Yogurt, Almond Butter Raspberries & Coconut	Fried Eggs with Avocado	
Lunch	**Lunch**	**Lunch**	
Caesar Salad	Chops Marinated in Red Pesto	Salmon & Broccoli Saute	
Dinner	**Dinner**	**Dinner**	
Thai Coconut Soup	Lemon Garlic Steak	Thai Coconut Soup	

EASY BREAKFAST
MENU...

Breakfast Menu:

Spinach Feta Scrambled Eggs - 13

Almond Cocoa Protein Smoothie - 15

Coconut / Almond Pancakes - 17

Omelet with Onions, Peppers & Cheese - 19

Avocado Mint Green Smoothie - 21

Yogurt, Almond Butter, Raspberries & Coconut - 23

Boiled Eggs & Avocado - 25

Coconut Almond Hot Cereal - 27

Fried Eggs & Crispy Bacon - 29

Fried Eggs With Avocado - 31

Spinach Feta Scrambled Eggs

Servings: 1	Time: 7 min

Nutritional Facts Per Serving:

Net Carbs:	6.8 g	Protein:	35 g
Fat:	44 g	Calories:	575 kcal

Ingredients:

3 large eggs

1 cup of spinach leaves

½ cup feta cheese

Salt

Black pepper

Drizzle of coconut oil

Directions:

While your pan is heating up. Grab a bowl and crack 3 eggs into it, add your spinach, feta, salt and pepper. Then whisk all together and pour into your pan. Scramble them up or leave to cook as an omelet, serve when ready.

Almond Cocoa Protein Smoothie

Servings: 1	Time: 5 min

Nutritional Facts Per Serving:
Net Carbs: 7.44 g   Protein: 17 g
Fat: 29 g   Calories: 337 kcal

Ingredients:

2 tbsp unsweetened almond butter

1 tbsp unsweetened cocoa powder

2 cups unsweetened almond milk

2 tbsp full fat yogurt

1 large egg

1 tsp Swerve (optional)

Directions:

Pour your almond milk, yogurt, egg, almond butter and cocoa into the blender and blend until well mixed and serve.

Coconut / Almond Pancakes

Coconut Pancakes

Servings: 5		Time: 30 min
Nutritional Facts Per Serving:		
Net Carbs:	2.6 g	Protein: 6.8 g
Fat:	17.6 g	Calories: 198 kcal

Almond Pancakes

Servings: 9		Time: 30 min
Nutritional Facts Per Serving:		
Carbs:	2.2 g	Protein: 5.9 g
Fat:	11.6 g	Calories: 142.4 kcal

Ingredients:

Coconut/ Almond Pancakes:

Coconut oil

¾ cup almond flour or ¼ cup coconut flour

4 large eggs

½ cup cream cheese

Vanilla extract, to taste

Few shakes of cinnamon

1 tbsp Swerve

1 tsp baking powder

Directions:

Put the cream cheese in a mixing bowl and into the microwave for about 10 seconds to make it soft. Pile on the rest of the ingredients and whisk until smooth. Let it settle for 10 minutes. Use ¼ cup to make sure they are all the same. Cook with some coconut oil and low and slow as these brown quickly. These can be modified with adding cocoa, raspberries, strawberries or pumpkin spices etc.

Omelet with Onions, Peppers & Cheese

Servings: 1	Time: 10 min

Nutritional Facts Per Serving:		
Net Carbs: 9.64 g	Protein:	46 g
Fat: 71 g	Calories:	867 kcal

Ingredients:

3 large eggs
1 tbsp heavy cream
1 slice onion, chopped
½ bell pepper, sliced (color of your choice)
1 cup cheddar cheese, grated
Salt
Black pepper
Drizzle of coconut oil

Directions:

Heat up your skillet with a drizzle of coconut oil on low to medium heat. In a mixing bowl, crack the eggs, cream, onion, bell pepper, salt and black pepper. Whisk it all together until it's fluffy. Pour mixture into pan, after 2 minutes sprinkle your cheese on top. When ready, fold half of the omelet over and serve.

Avocado Mint Green Smoothie

Servings: 1		Time: 5 min
Nutritional Facts Per Serving:		
Net Carbs: 13.58 g	Protein:	5.6 g
Fat:	48 g	Calories: 492 kcal

Ingredients:

½ of an avocado

¾ cup full fat coconut milk

½ cup almond milk

Swerve to taste

5 to 6 large mint leaves

3 sprigs of cilantro

1 squeeze of lime juice

¼ tsp vanilla

Directions:

Place all of the ingredients into the blender. Blend on low speed until completely pureed. Taste to adjust sweetness and tartness. Serve.

Yogurt, Almond Butter, Raspberry & Coconut

Servings: 1	Time: 2 min
Nutritional Facts Per Serving:	
Net Carbs: 32.24 g Protein: 24 g	
Fat: 35 g Calories: 541 kcal	

Ingredients:

1 cup of full fat yogurt

2 tbsp unsweetened almond butter

¼ cup raspberries

1 tbsp coconut flakes

Directions:

Pour yogurt into a bowl, add almond butter and mix together. Then add your raspberries and coconut flakes. Eat and enjoy!

Boiled Eggs & Avocado

Servings: 1		Time: 8 min
Nutritional Facts Per Serving:		
Net Carbs: 3.22 g	Protein:	15 g
Fat: 44 g	Calories:	489 kcal

Ingredients:

2 large eggs

1 avocado

Salt

Pepper

Drizzle of olive oil

Directions:

Boil two eggs, 5 minutes for a more runny egg or 7 minutes for a harder egg. Cut the avocado in half and scoop out with spoon, drizzle olive oil on top. Peel eggs once cooled. Add salt and pepper to your taste.

Coconut Almond Hot Cereal

Servings: 1	Time: 7 min
Nutritional Facts Per Serving:	
Net Carbs: 5.24 g Protein: 11 g	
Fat: 50 g Calories: 521 kcal	

Ingredients:

2 tbsp almond flour

2 tbsp flaxseed meal

2 tbsp dried unsweetened coconut, finely shredded

1 pinch of salt

1 tbsp almond butter

⅓ cup boiling water

¼ cup heavy cream

Swerve to taste

Directions:

We are going to mix all the dry ingredients together, add 1 tbsp of almond butter and the boiling water. Mix all together. Cover bowl to sit for 2 to 3 minutes. Add ¼ cup of heavy cream or coconut milk and the sweetener of your choice. Stir and enjoy!

Fried Eggs & Crispy Bacon

Servings: 1	Time: 10 min

Nutritional Facts Per Serving:
Net Carbs: 1.67 g   Protein: 31 g
Fat: 26 g   Calories: 376 kcal

Ingredients:

3 large eggs
3 bacon strips
Salt
Black pepper

Directions:

Heat up skillet on low to medium heat. Lay in the bacon and fry on both sides. Crack in and fry the eggs. Salt and pepper to taste.

Fried Eggs With Avocado

Servings: 1	Time: 8 min
Nutritional Facts Per Serving:	
Net Carbs: 3.22 g Protein: 15 g	
Fat: 44 g Calories: 489 kcal	

Ingredients:

1 avocado

2 large eggs

1 tbsp olive oil

Directions:

Heat up pan on low to medium with some olive oil. Slice your avocado in half, remove pip and carefully scoop out the avocado halves. Now slice each half of your avocado so it has a hole in the center of each slice. Use these two slices to put into the skillet. Then crack open each egg and place into the middle of the avocado holes, fry until ready to serve. Use the left over avocado to add to your meal.

EASY LUNCH MENU...

Lunch Menu:

Bacon, Avocado Egg Salad - 35

Sliced Steak with Brussels Sprouts - 37

Lettuce Hamburger Beef Patty - 39

Zesty Lime Shrimp & Avocado Salad - 41

Chicken Wings, Celery Sticks & Dip Nut - 43

Chops Marinated in Red Pesto - 45

Avocado Tuna Salad - 47

Caesar Salad - 49

Garlic Chicken Zoodles - 51

Salmon & Broccoli Saute - 53

Bacon, Avocado & Egg Salad

Servings: 1	Time: 10 min

Nutritional Facts Per Serving:
Net Carbs: 6.57 g   Protein: 33 g
Fat: 64 g   Calories: 766 kcal

Ingredients:

3 bacon strips

1 avocado

2 large eggs

Bowl of lettuce

Half a cucumber

¼ cup feta cheese

1 tbsp olive oil

Directions:

Heat up your skillet on low to medium heat. Boil a small pot of water for your eggs. Place the bacon in skillet and cook until crispy. Wash the lettuce and cucumber you will be using in your salad. Chop up some cucumber and lettuce to fit into your bowl. Sprinkle some feta on top. Once the boiled eggs have cooled down after boiling, peel them and cut them up into quarters, put these into your salad. Then take your bacon when cooled after cooking and place them into your salad. Add a drizzle of olive oil and squeeze in some lemon for flavor.

Sliced Steak with Brussels Sprouts

Servings: 1		Time: 35 min
Nutritional Facts Per Serving:		
Net Carbs: 8.4 g	Protein:	52.6 g
Fat: 41.9 g	Calories:	869 kcal

Ingredients:

3 tbsp butter

2 spring onions, chopped

1 medium skirt steak

Salt

Black pepper

1 cup Brussels sprouts, cut in half

1½ tsp olive oil

Directions:

Directions: Preheat a large cast-iron skillet on high heat. Meanwhile, in a small bowl, whip butter and chopped up spring onions. Set aside. Rinse and pat dry the steak with a paper towel. Season generously with salt and pepper. When cast iron pan is hot, add ½ teaspoon olive oil to pan and the steak. Sear on high for 3 minutes each side. Remove and add ½ tablespoon of spring onion butter over the steak. Cover loosely with foil and let rest. In a mixing bowl, combine Brussels sprouts and 1 tablespoon olive oil. Season with ½ teaspoon salt and ¼ teaspoon pepper. In the same pan, sear Brussels sprouts, until golden brown, about 5 minutes. (If you want a crispier texture, add more olive oil and cook a few more minutes.) Slice steak against the grain and serve with remaining butter.

Lettuce Hamburger Beef Patty

Servings: 1	Time: 20 min

Nutritional Facts Per Serving:
Net Carbs: 3.01 g   Protein: 29 g
Fat: 45 g   Calories: 551 kcal

Ingredients:

Ground beef patty

Large iceberg lettuce leaf

Slice of tomato

Cheddar cheese, sliced

Half an avocado, sliced

Salt

Black pepper

Two sprigs of cilantro

Drizzle of olive oil

Directions:

Heat up the skillet at medium heat with some olive oil. Once heated place your burger patty in. Flip over once it is crispy brown. Take your washed lettuce leaf and place it on your plate, when both sides of your beef patty are cooked place it in the lettuce leaf bowl. Then place your sliced tomato, sliced cheese, avocado slices and cilantro on top. Add your salt and pepper to your liking and enjoy!

Zesty Lime Shrimp & Avocado Salad

Servings: 4	Time: 10 min

Nutritional Facts Per Serving:
Net Carbs: 7.12 g   Protein: 27.25 g
Fat: 8.5 g   Calories: 224.5 kcal

Ingredients:

¼ cup chopped red onion
Juice of 2 small limes
1 tsp olive oil
¼ tsp salt
Black pepper
1 lb jumbo shrimp, peeled and cooked, cut into bite-size pieces
1 medium avocado, chopped
1 medium tomato, chopped
1 fresh jalapeño pepper, seeded and finely chopped
1 tbsp cilantro, fresh, chopped

Directions:

In a small bowl, combine the onion, lime juice, olive oil, salt, and pepper
to taste. Let sit for at least 5 minutes. In a large bowl, combine the shrimp,
avocado, tomato, and jalapeño. Add the onion mixture and the cilantro, and toss
gently. Season with pepper, if desired.

Chicken Wings, Celery Sticks & Nut Dip

Servings: 2	Time: 45 min
Nutritional Facts Per Serving:	
Net Carbs: 3 g	Protein: 85 g
Fat: 80 g	Calories: 1095 kcal

Ingredients:

1 ½ lb chicken wing segments (flats and drums)

2 tbsp olive oil

3 tsp of all purpose seasoning (your favorite)

2 celery sticks, washed

2 tbsp almond butter

Directions:

Preheat oven to 390°F. Line a baking tray with foil and then place a cooling rack inside the baking tray. In a small bowl combine the olive oil and the seasoning and stir till combined. Pat the chicken wing segments dry with some paper towel and place them in a large bowl. Pour the seasoned olive oil over the chicken segments and toss until they are all completely coated. We find this is easiest using our hands. Place the wings on the rack over the tray, space them evenly so the air can circulate around them. Place in the oven for 40 to 45 minutes until they are golden brown and the skin is crispy.

Serve with your sliced celery sticks and almond butter dip.

Chops Marinated in Red Pesto

Servings: 1	Time: 15 min

Nutritional Facts Per Serving:
Net Carbs: 1.18 g   Protein: 42 g
Fat: 50 g   Calories: 634 kcal

Ingredients:

1 pork chop

½ tbsp butter or olive oil

1 tbsp red pesto

Pesto mayonnaise:

2 tbsp keto friendly mayonnaise

½ tbsp red pesto

Salad:

Broccoli

Cauliflower

Cheese

Arugula

Directions:

Rub the chops with pesto and fry on medium heat in butter or oil for 8 minutes and let simmer for 4 more minutes on low heat. Mix mayonnaise with red pesto. Serve on the side. Mix your broccoli & cauliflower in cheese and add arugula for your salad.

Avocado Tuna Salad

Servings: 4	Time: 10 min

Nutritional Facts Per Serving:
Net Carbs: 2.67 g Protein: 10.5 g
Fat: 10 g Calories: 152.25 kcal

Ingredients:

1 can tuna packed in water or oil, drained
1 ripe avocado, roughly chopped
½ cup cucumber, chopped
¼ cup celery, minced
¼ cup onion, red or green, minced
2 tbsp cilantro or parsley, chopped fresh
1 tbsp olive oil
1 tbsp lemon juice
½ tsp salt
Black pepper

Directions:

Place all of the ingredients in a medium bowl. Mix with a fork or spoon until the avocado is roughly mashed and mixed through. Serve on lettuce wraps (optional).

Caesar Salad

Servings: 2	Time: 30 min
Nutritional Facts Per Serving:	
Net Carbs: 6.33 g Protein: 66 g	
Fat: 28 g Calories: 558.5 kcal	

Ingredients:

¾ lb chicken breasts

1 tbsp olive oil

Salt

Black pepper

4 bacon strips

½ lb romaine lettuce

2 tbsp parmesan cheese, grated

Dressing

1 tbsp Dijon mustard

½ lemon, zest and juice

2 tbsp parmesan cheese, grated

2 tbsp fillets of anchovies, finely chopped

1 clove of garlic, pressed or finely chopped (optional)

Salt

Black pepper

Directions:

Mix the ingredients for the dressing with a whisk or an immersion blender. Set aside in the refrigerator. Preheat the oven to 400°F. Place the chicken breasts in a greased baking dish. Season the chicken with salt and pepper and drizzle olive oil or melted butter on top. Bake the chicken in the oven for about 20 minutes or until fully cooked through. You can also cook the chicken on the stove top if you prefer. Fry the bacon until crisp. Shred the lettuce and place as a base on two plates. Place sliced chicken and the crispy, crumbled bacon on top. Finish with a generous dollop of dressing and a good grating of parmesan cheese.

Garlic Chicken Zoodles

Servings: 2	Time: 15 min

Nutritional Facts Per Serving:
Net Carbs: 11 g Protein: 41.5 g
Fat: 19 g Calories: 376.5 kcal

Ingredients:

2 medium chicken breasts cut into ½ inch pieces
2 tbsp olive oil
4 clove of garlic, minced or crushed
3 zucchini spiralized (zoodles)
5 florets of broccoli
½ tsp red pepper flakes (optional)
Salt
Black pepper

Directions:

Preheat a large, heavy pan to medium-high heat. Add olive oil and garlic. Cook garlic for 30 seconds to 1 minute. Add chicken, red pepper flakes, salt and black pepper. Cook chicken for 5 to 6 minutes or until golden and cooked through. Toss in spiralized zoodles and cook for 1 minute then turn off heat. (Sprinkle with parmesan cheese if desired.)

Salmon & Broccoli Saute

Servings: 4	Time: 10 min

Nutritional Facts Per Serving:
Net Carbs: 3.17 g   Protein: 71.5 g
Fat: 54.25 g   Calories: 806 kcal

Ingredients:

4 tbsp of avocado oil, for cooking
6 cloves of garlic, minced or finely diced
2 tbsp of fresh ginger, minced or finely diced
4 eggs, whisked
1 head of broccoli (1 lb), chopped small
¾ salmon, diced
2 tbsp of gluten-free tamari sauce or coconut aminos (optional)
Salt
Black pepper

Directions:

In a large skillet over medium-high heat, add the avocado oil. Add the garlic and ginger to the skillet and saute until fragrant, about 30 seconds. Add the eggs to the skillet and saute until almost cooked, about 1 to 2 minutes. Add the broccoli to the skillet and saute until slightly softened, about 5 to 6 minutes. Add the salmon and optional coconut aminos to the skillet and saute until the salmon is cooked through, about 2 to 4 minutes. Season with salt and pepper, to taste. (Optional) If your salmon has skin on it, then remove the skin and fry it in some avocado oil on high heat for 2 to 3 minutes until crispy. Place on some paper towels to soak up the excess oil and enjoy with the saute.

EASY-DINNER MENU...

Dinner Menu:

Garlic Chicken with Broccoli & Spinach - 57

Grilled Salmon with Avocado & Salsa - 59

Chicken Taco Lettuce Wraps - 61

Garlic Shrimp Zucchini Pasta - 63

Garlic Steak Bites - 65

Sesame Salmon with Baby Bok Choy & Mushrooms - 67

Pesto Chicken & Veggies - 69

Stir -Fry Chicken & Veggies - 71

Thai Chicken Soup - 73

Lemon Garlic Steak - 75

Garlic Chicken with Broccoli & Spinach

Servings: 4   Time: 15 min

Nutritional Facts Per Serving:
Net Carbs: 6.74 g Protein: 42.75 g
Fat: 24.25 g Calories: 430.25 kcal

Ingredients:

1 lb chicken breasts, cut into 1-inch pieces
2 tbsp olive oil
1 tsp Italian seasoning
¼ tsp pepper, crushed (optional)
Salt
Black pepper
3 to 4 cloves of garlic, minced
½ cup red bell peppers, chopped
2 cups broccoli florets
2 cups baby spinach
½ cup shredded cheese. (Can be mozzarella, cheddar, parmesan, or choose your favorite cheese for melting)
½ cup cream cheese

Directions:

Heat 2 tablespoons olive oil in a large saucepan over medium-high heat. Add the chopped chicken breasts, season with Italian seasoning, crushed red pepper, salt and black pepper. Sauté for 4 to 5 minutes or until chicken is golden and cooked through. Add the garlic and sauté for another minute. Add the red bell peppers, broccoli, spinach, shredded cheese, and cream cheese. Cook for another 3 to 4 minutes or until the broccoli is cooked through. Serve with cooked zucchini noodles or cauliflower rice if you wish.

Grilled Salmon with Avocado & Salsa

Servings: 2	Time: 22 min
Nutritional Facts Per Serving:	
Net Carbs: 5.49 g Protein: 52.5 g	
Fat: 59 g Calories: 785 kcal	

Ingredients:

2 salmon fillets

2 tbsp olive oil

1 clove of garlic, minced or crushed

½ tsp chili powder

½ tsp cumin

½ tsp onion powder

¼ tsp black pepper

¼ tsp salt

The avocado salsa

1 ripe avocado, pitted and diced

½ cup tomato, diced

2 tbsp onion, diced

2 tbsp cilantro, minced

1 tbsp olive oil

1 tbsp lime juice

Salt

Black pepper

Directions:

Stir the olive oil, garlic, and spices in a small bowl. Brush or rub salmon with the spice mixture. Preheat a large, heavy skillet or grill to medium-high heat. Add salmon to the skillet and cook for 5 to 6 minutes per side. Remove from pan, top with avocado salsa and serve immediately. To make the avocado salsa: Add the avocado, tomato, onion, and cilantro to a large mixing bowl. Drizzle with olive oil, fresh lime juice and a pinch of salt and pepper. Gently mix with a spoon until fully combined. To bake salmon: preheat oven to 400°F. Place salmon on a sheet pan and bake for 12 to 15 minutes or until cooked through.

Chicken Taco Lettuce Wraps

Servings: 4	Time: 30 min

Nutritional Facts Per Serving:
Net Carbs: 7.5 g   Protein: 40 g
Fat: 19.75 g   Calories:388.75 kcal

Ingredients:

Grilled taco chicken

1 lb boneless, skinless chicken breasts or thighs

2 tbsp taco seasoning

2 cloves of garlic, minced

1 tbsp olive oil

To Assemble

8 leaves romaine lettuce, rinsed

1 avocado, diced

1 tomato, diced

¼ cup onion, diced

Cilantro sauce

½ cup loosely packed cilantro

½ cup Greek yogurt or sour cream or mayonnaise

2 tbsp olive oil

1 jalapeño (optional)

1 clove of garlic, minced

Juice of ½ lime

Pinch of salt

Directions:

To cook the chicken: add the chicken, garlic, olive oil, and spices in a large bowl or zip seal bag. Place in refrigerator and let marinate for at least 15 to 30 minutes or up to 24 hours. Remove chicken from marinade and discard marinade. Place chicken on a grill or pan preheated to medium-high heat. Let chicken cook until it is no longer pink on the inside, about 9 to 10 minutes per side or until it has reached an internal temperature of 165°F. To make the cilantro sauce, place all the ingredients in the food processor and blend for 1 minute or until creamy. Layer lettuce wraps with chicken, tomatoes, onion, and avocado. Drizzle with cilantro sauce or your favorite taco sauce.

Garlic Shrimp Zucchini Pasta

Servings: 4	Time: 15 min

Nutritional Facts Per Serving:
Net Carbs: 5.88 g   Protein: 18.5 g
Fat: 11.5 g   Calories: 204 kcal

Ingredients:

3 - 4 medium zucchini

1 lb raw shrimp, peeled and deveined

1 tbsp olive oil

2 tbsp butter

3 - 4 garlic cloves, minced or crushed

1 tsp Italian seasoning or oregano, optional

¼ tsp of red pepper flakes

Salt and pepper to taste

Freshly grated parmesan or chopped parsley to garnish, optional

Directions:

Wash and trim the ends of the zucchini. Make the zucchini noodles using a spiralizer and set aside. Heat 1 tablespoon oil in a large skillet over medium-high heat. Add the shrimp to the hot pan, season with salt and pepper cook for 1 minute. Add the garlic, Italian seasoning, and crushed pepper to the pan. Cook for another minute per side or until shrimp is light pink and garlic is golden brown. Transfer to a bowl. Add the butter and zucchini noodles to the same pan, season with salt and pepper. Cook for 2 minutes or until tender. Return the cooked shrimp to the pan and stir through. Garnished with freshly grated parmesan cheese or/and chopped parsley.

Garlic Steak Bites

Servings: 4	Time: 20 min

Nutritional Facts Per Serving:
Net Carbs: 0.93 g   Protein: 61.5 g
Fat: 41.5 g   Calories: 636.25 kcal

Ingredients:

2 lb sirloin steak, cut into 1-inch cubes

1 tbsp olive oil

2 tbsp butter

3 - 4 cloves of garlic, minced or crushed

Salt

Black pepper

Directions:

Heat oil in a large, heavy skillet or cast iron pan for at least 1 minute. Generously season the steak with salt and pepper. Place the steak in the pan in a single layer without overcrowding the pan (work in batches if needed). Cook for 2 minutes per side or until seared and dark brown. Remove the steak from the pan and add the butter and garlic to the pan. Stir for 30 seconds or until the garlic is light brown. Pour garlic over steak bites and enjoy with some salad (optional).

Sesame Salmon, Baby Bok Choy & Mushrooms

Servings: 4   Time: 30 min

Nutritional Facts Per Serving:
Net Carbs: 8 g   Protein: 62 g
Fat: 34.75 g   Calories: 616.25 kcal

Ingredients:

Main Dish

4 salmon fillet

8 mushrooms

16 baby bok choy

1 tbsp toasted sesame seeds

4 green onion

Marinade

1 tbsp olive oil

1 tsp sesame oil

1 tbsp coconut aminos

1 tsp ginger, grated

1 tsp lemon juice

½ tsp salt

½ tsp black pepper

Directions:

Whisk together all of your marinade ingredients. Drizzle half of the marinade on the salmon and turn to coat. Cover and refrigerate the salmon while it marinates for one hour. Preheat oven to 400. Prepare vegetables: Trim the rough ends from the bok choy and cut into halves. Slice the mushrooms into ½ inch pieces. Drizzle the remaining marinade over the vegetables and lay on a lined baking sheet. Place salmon, skin side down, on a lined baking sheet as well. Bake until salmon is cooked through, about 20 minutes. Top with sliced green onions and sesame seeds. Serve with grilled or steamed veggies, or a salad.

Pesto Chicken & Veggies

Servings: 4	Time: 25 min

Nutritional Facts Per Serving:
Net Carbs: 6.48 g Protein: 37.75 g
Fat: 15 g Calories: 324.75 kcal

Ingredients:

4 chicken fillets, chop into bite-size pieces
1 cup broccoli florets
1 bell pepper, chopped
1 large zucchini, chopped
¼ cup basil pesto
½ cup mozzarella cheese (optional)

Directions:

Preheat oven to 425°F. In a large bowl, combine the chicken, veggies, and pesto. Mix until the chicken and veggies are coated well with pesto. Transfer mixture to a large sheet pan and bake for 15 to 20 minutes. If desired drizzle with mozzarella cheese during the last 5 minutes of baking.

Stir-Fry Chicken & Veggies

Servings: 4	Time: 20 min
Nutritional Facts Per Serving:	
Net Carbs: 8.56 g Protein: 33.5 g	
Fat: 11 g Calories: 281 kcal	

Ingredients:

2 tbsp olive oil

4 chicken breast fillets, cut into ½-inch thick slices

2 cups broccoli florets

1 large zucchini, cut into slices

1 medium bell peppers, cut into ½-inch thick slices

1 medium yellow onion, halved and cut into ½-inch thick slices

½ cup mushrooms

3 - 4 cloves of garlic, minced or crushed

1 tbsp Italian seasoning (or your favorite seasoning blend)

1 tsp salt

½ tsp black pepper

Directions:

Heat 2 tablespoons oil in large skillet to medium-high heat. Add the chicken, veggies, garlic, and spices. Cook for 8 to 10 minutes, stirring occasionally until the veggies are soft and tender and the chicken is golden and cooked through.

Thai Chicken Soup

Servings: 3	Time: 35 min

Nutritional Facts Per Serving:
Net Carbs:	3.19 g	Protein:	26.67 g
Fat:	11 g	Calories:	220 kcal

Ingredients:

2 large chicken breasts
½ cup coconut milk
½ cup chicken broth
2 cups water
2 tbsp Red Boat fish sauce
1 tbsp Thai garlic chili paste
1 tsp coconut aminos
1 tsp lime juice
½ tsp ground ginger
1 fresh sprig of Thai basil
Cilantro, to garnish

Directions:

Thinly slice chicken breast into quarter inch thick strips, then cut once more to make the pieces of chicken bite-sized. In a large stock pot, combine coconut milk, broth, water, fish sauce, chili sauce, coconut aminos, lime juice, ginger, and basil. Bring to a boil over high heat. Stir in chicken pieces, reduce heat to low to medium, and cover pot; simmer for 30 minutes. Remove basil leaves from the soup and garnish with cilantro.

Lemon Garlic Steak

Servings: 4	Time: 11 min
Nutritional Facts Per Serving:	
Net Carbs: 2.23 g Protein: 127.5 g	
Fat: 90 g Calories: 1327 kcal	

Ingredients:

4 ½-inch thick, top chuck blade steaks

1 tsp salt

½ tsp black pepper

½ tsp paprika, optional

2 tbsp unsalted butter

1 tbsp olive oil

4 garlic cloves, 2 diced and 2 whole for pan

Juice of 1 lemon

4 asparagus, wash and trim

Directions:

Pat steaks dry and sprinkle both sides with salt, pepper, diced garlic and a squeeze of lemon. Heat 1 tablespoon butter, olive oil and garlic in a 12-inch heavy skillet over medium-high heat until hot but not smoking. Add steaks then sauté 2 to 3 minutes per side for medium. Squeeze more lemon juice on the steak right before removing from heat. Cook the asparagus and serve with your steak.

YUMMY EXTRAS...

FEW EASY DESSERTS

Dessert Menu:

Peanut Butter Fluff Fat Bomb - 79

Chocolate Mousse - 81

Chocolate Peanut Butter Bark - 83

Raspberry Almond Chocolate Fat Bomb - 85

Chocolate Coconut Almond Fat Bombs - 87

Peanut Butter Fluff Fat Bomb

Servings: 6

Nutritional Facts Per Serving:
Net Carbs: 10.24 g   Protein: 3.67 g
Fat: 18.17 g   Calories: 187.5 kcal

Ingredients:

½ cup heavy whipping cream (about 1 cup whipped)

4 oz cream cheese, softened

2 ¼ tbsp natural peanut butter

5 tbsp Swerve, confectioners

½ tsp vanilla

½ square unsweetened chocolate

Directions:

In a medium-sized bowl, beat heavy whipping cream until it almost doubles in size. In a separate bowl add the softened cream cheese, natural peanut butter, Swerve and vanilla. Beat with a mixer until the fluff is smooth and creamy. Combine the two and mix on low until thoroughly combined and smooth. Grate unsweetened chocolate shavings on top. Best if kept in the refrigerator overnight and served the next day.

Chocolate Mousse

Servings: 4

Nutritional Facts Per Serving:
Net Carbs: 1.63 g   Protein: 1.6 g
Fat: 21.5 g   Calories: 203 kcal

Ingredients:

4 tbsp unsalted butter

4 tbsp cream cheese

¼ cup heavy whipping cream

1 tbsp cacao powder

Swerve, to taste

Directions:

Soften butter and combine with Swerve, stirring until completely blended. Add cream cheese; blend until smooth. Add cacao powder and blend completely. Whip heavy cream and gradually add it to the mixture. (You may also add 1 teaspoon of coconut oil or MCT oil). Spoon into small glasses and refrigerate for 30 minutes.

Chocolate Peanut Butter Bark

Servings: 25   Time: 1 h

Nutritional Facts Per Serving:
Net Carbs:	1.32 g	Protein: 1.68 g
Fat:	12.56 g	Calories: 126.5 kcal

Ingredients:

1 cup coconut oil

¼ cup unsweetened cacao powder

½ cup natural peanut butter, creamy

½ cup Swerve

¼ tsp salt

1 tsp vanilla extract

1 tsp almond extract

½ cup shredded coconut, unsweetened

Directions:

Melt the coconut oil and peanut butter. Stir until creamy and no chunks of coconut oil remain. Add the sea salt, Swerve, shredded coconut, almond extract, vanilla extract, and cacao powder. Mix well. Line a baking sheet with parchment paper. Pour the melted chocolate on the pan. Freeze the chocolate for 45 minutes. Break into pieces & store in a closed container in the freezer.

Raspberry Almond Chocolate Fat Bomb Bark

Servings: 8	Time: 1 h 5 min

Nutritional Facts Per Serving:
Net Carbs: 2.7 g   Protein: 3.88 g
Fat: 17.63 g   Calories: 189 kcal

Ingredients:

¼ cup almond butter

½ cup coconut butter

1 tbsp unsweetened cocoa powder

¼ tsp Swerve, confectioners

⅛ cup raw almonds

⅛ cup walnuts

¼ cup raspberries

Directions:

In a bowl, mix together the coconut butter, almond butter, Swerve powder and cocoa powder. Chop the almonds and walnuts. Heat the raspberries for 40 to 60 seconds. Place some parchment paper over a square pan and pour the chocolate butter inside. Sprinkle the nuts over and cover with the softened raspberries. Place in the freezer for minimum one hour to freeze. Take it out and break it into 8 pieces (or more if you want smaller portions). Always keep frozen. You can transfer the chocolate pieces to a Tupperware after it's frozen.

Chocolate Coconut Almond Fat Bombs

Servings: 30	Time: 1 h 10 min

Nutritional Facts Per Serving:
Net Carbs: 1.03 g   Protein: 0.93 g
Fat: 8.13 g   Calories: 84.27 kcal

Ingredients:

½ cup coconut oil, melted

½ cup coconut butter, melted

¼ cup cacao powder

1 tsp almond extract

½ tsp vanilla extract

½ tsp Swerve, confectioners

¼ cup almonds, chopped

¼ cup unsweetened coconut, finely shredded

¼ cup cacao nibs

Directions:

Heat the Swerve on the stove for 1 to 2 minutes until fully dissolved.
Mix coconut oil, coconut butter, cacao powder, almond extract, vanilla extract
and Swerve together. Add in chopped almonds, coconut flakes, and cacao
nibs. With a tablespoon, fill mini cupcake liners or an ice cube tray, putting 1
tablespoonful in each. Store in refrigerator.

FEW

EASY

DRINKS..

Drinks Menu:

Hot Buttery Coffee - 91

Iced Tea - 93

Flavored Water - 95

Pumpkin Spice Latte - 97

Hot Chocolate - 99

Hot Buttery Coffee

Servings: 1

Nutritional Facts Per Serving:
| Net Carbs: | 0 g | Protein: | 0.5 g |
| Fat: | 37 g | Calories: | 327 kcal |

Ingredients:

1 cup hot coffee, freshly brewed

2 tbsp unsalted butter

1 tbsp MCT oil or coconut oil

Directions:

Combine all ingredients in a blender. Blend until smooth and frothy. Serve immediately.

Iced Tea

Servings: 2

Nutritional Facts Per Serving:			
Net Carbs:	0.49 g	Protein:	0.05 g
Fat:	0 g	Calories:	1.9 kcal

Ingredients:

2 cups cold water
1 tea bag (tea of your choice)
1 cup of ice cubes
Flavorings of your choice, such as sliced lemon or fresh mint

Directions:

Combine the tea, flavoring and half of the cold water into a pitcher. Leave in the refrigerator for 1 to 2 hours. Remove the tea bag and the flavoring. Replace with new, fresh flavoring if you so desire. Add the rest of the cold water and serve with lots of ice cubes.

Flavored Water

Servings: 2			
Nutritional Facts Per Serving:			
Net Carbs:	0 g	Protein:	0 g
Fat:	0 g	Calories:	0 kcal

Ingredients:

4 cups fresh, cold water

Flavoring of your choice: fresh raspberries/fresh mint/sliced cucumber/lemon

2 cups of ice cubes

Directions:

Pour fresh, cold water into a pitcher. Add flavoring of your choice and let sit in the fridge for at least 30 minutes. Possible additions include berries, fruit, fresh mint, or citrus fruits like orange, grapefruit, lime and lemon in thin slices. Cucumber is another classic with a neutral but refreshing taste.

Pumpkin Spice Latte

Servings: 1		
Nutritional Facts Per Serving:		
Net Carbs: 2.46 g	Protein:	0.6 g
Fat: 25 g	Calories:	228 kcal

Ingredients:

2 tbsp unsalted butter

1 tsp pumpkin pie spice

1 - 2 tsp instant coffee powder

1 cup boiling water

Directions:

Place butter, spices and instant coffee (shot of espresso or even decaf) in a deep bowl to use with an immersion blender. Alternatively, you can put the ingredients directly into the jar of a blender. Add boiling water and blend for 20 to 30 seconds until a fine foam has formed. Pour into a cup and sprinkle some cinnamon or pumpkin spice on top. Serve immediately! It's even more delicious with a dollop of whipped heavy cream on top.

Hot Chocolate

Servings: 1

Nutritional Facts Per Serving:
Net Carbs: 2.57 g   Protein: 1.3 g
Fat: 24 g   Calories: 229 kcal

Ingredients:

2 tbsp unsalted butter

1 tbsp cocoa powder

1 tsp Swerve, confectioners (optional)

¼ tsp vanilla extract

1 cup boiling water

Directions:

Put the ingredients in a tall beaker to use with an immersion blender. Mix for 15 to 20 seconds or until there's a fine foam on top. Pour the hot cocoa into a cup and enjoy.

SHOPPING LIST:

BEEF

- Steak
- Prime Rib
- Veal
- Roast Beef
- Brisket
- Loin
- Ground beef
- Stew meats
- Organs

POULTRY

- Chicken
- Quail
- Turkey
- Organs
- Eggs

PORK

- Bacon
- Ground pork
- Sausage
- Bratwurst
- Pork rinds
- Ham
- Pork chops

SEAFOOD

- Salmon
- Tuna
- Trout
- Cod
- Sardines
- Tilapia
- Shrimp
- Lobster
- Crab
- Bass
- Scallops
- Mussels
- Clams
- Oysters

OTHER • Deli meats • Jerky sticks • Biltong • Salami • Goat • Lamb

LEAFY GREENS

- Spinach
- Kale
- Swiss chard
- Lettuce
- Bok choy
- Watercress
- Endive
- Dandelion greens

CRUCIFEROUS VEGGIES

- Broccoli
- Cauliflower
- Red cabbage
- Green cabbage
- Napa cabbage
- Brussels sprouts

ALL OTHER VEGETABLES AND GREENS

- Avocado
- Asparagus
- Celery
- Spring onion
- Fennel
- Radish
- Kohlrabi
- Jalapeño peppers
- Zucchini
- Eggplant
- Green peppers
- Other bell peppers
- Cucumbers
- Tomatoes
- Spaghetti squash
- Sauerkraut
- White mushrooms
- Portobello mushrooms
- Beetroot
- Brown onion
- Red onion
- Carrots
- Bean sprouts
- Artichoke
- Ginger
- Garlic
- Olives
- Basil
- Sage
- Parsley
- Chives
- Dill

FRUITS AND BERRIES

- Raspberries
- Blackberries
- Strawberries
- Coconut
- Lemon
- Lime
- Starfruit

FATS AND OILS

- Coconut oil • Olive oil • Avocado oil • MCT oil • Grass fed butter

DAIRY

- Greek yogurt
- Kefir
- Heavy cream
- Half n' Half
- Feta
- Mozzarella
- Cheddar
- Blue cheese
- Parmesan
- Cottage cheese
- Swiss cheese
- Gouda
- Cream cheese
- Colby
- Ricotta
- Brie
- Goat cheese
- Sour cream

DRINKS

- Spring water
- Sparkling water
- Tea
- Coffee
- Bone broth
- Keto greens
- MCT powder mix
- Coconut milk
- Almond milk

CONDIMENTS AND SAUCES

- Apple cider vinegar
- Balsamic vinegar
- Mustard
- Ketchup (sugar free)
- Avocado Mayonnaise
- Salsa
- Lemon juice
- Horseradish
- Lime juice
- Hot sauces
- Soy sauce
- Tabasco

HERBS AND SPICES

- Apple cider vinegar
- Himalayan pink salt
- Sea salt
- Black pepper
- Cilantro
- Cinnamon
- Turmeric
- Cayenne
- Cumin
- Basil
- Thyme
- Sage
- Oregano
- Dill
- Rosemary
- Chili powder
- Paprika

SWEETNERS		CHOCOLATE
- Monk Fruit - Xylitol - Lakanto - Swerve	- Erythritol - Stevia - Pyure - Truvia	- Cocoa Powder - Cacoa Powder - Sugar Free Cooking Chocolate - Dark Chocolate

FLOURS

- Almond Meal
- Almond Flour
- Coconut flour
- Ground Hazelnut flour
- Ground Macadamia flour
- Ground Peanut flour
- Ground Chai Seeds
- Flaxseed Meal
- Sunflower seed meal

THICKENING AGENTS

- Oat Fiber
- Psyllium Husks
- Gelatin
- Glucomannan
- Collagen Protein Powder
- Inulin
- Xanthan gum

KETO FRIENDLY FOOD LIST:

VEGETABLES PART 1

 0.3g
Endive

 0.6g
Beet greens

 0.7g
Chicory

 0.8g
Watercress

 1.2g
Pak choi (bok choy)

 1.4g
Kale (cavolo nero)

 1.4g
Spinach

 1.4g
Celery

 1.4g
Collard

 1.5g
Cucumber

 1.5g
Samphire

 1.5g
Mustard greens

 1.7g
Parsley root
(not parsnip!)

 1.8g
Asparagus

1.8g
Radishes

 1.8g
Mizuna greens

 1-2g
Lettuce

2.1g
Swiss chard

2.1g
Zucchini (courgette)

2.1g
Arugula (rocket)

 2.3g
White mushroom

 2.6g
Napa cabbage

 2.6g
Potobello mushroom

2.6g
Kohlrabi

 2.7g
Tomatoes

 2.9g
Green bell pepper

 2.9g
Eggplant (aubergine)

   3g
Savoy cabbage

  3g
Cauliflower

 3.2g
Green cabbage

| BEST | ← CARBS → | WORST |

VEGETABLES PART 2

 3.3g
White Cabbage

 3.6g
Radicchio

 3.6g
Kale (curly)

 3.7g
Jalapeno peppers

 3.9g
Other bell pepper

 3.8g
Oyster mushroom

 3.9g
Jicama

 4g
Bean sprouts

 4g
Broccoli

 4g
Daikon radish

 4.2g
Fennel

 4.3g
Green beans

 4.3g
Shiitake mushroom

 4.6g
Turnip

 4.7g
Spring Onion

 5.1g
Artichoke (globe)

 5.2g
Brussel sprouts

 5.3g
Red cabbage

 5.4g
Spaghetti squash

 5.7g
Dandelion greens

 6g
Pie pumpkin

 6.3g
Rutabaga (swede)

 6.4g
Brown onion

 6.5g
Red onion

6.8g
Carrot

 6.8g
Beetroot

 7g
Celeriac

 7g
Hokkaido squash

7.6g
White onion

 9.7g
Butter squash

| BEST | ← CARBS → | WORST |

DRINKS

Water with lemon — 0, 1 cup

Tea — 0, 1 cup

Coffee — 0, 1 cup

Coconut water — 9, 1 cup

Vegetable juice — 11*, 1 cup

Milk — 11*, 1 cup

Soy milk — 12*, 1 cup

Caffè latte — 15, 12 oz

Orange juice — 26, 1 cup

Energy drink — 28, 8.4 oz

Ice tea — 32, 12 oz

Smoothie — 36, 1 cup

Soft drink — 39, 12 oz

Frappuccino — 50, 12 oz

Milkshake — 60, 10 oz

BEST ← CARBS → WORST

CONDIMENTS AND MORE

 0
1 cup
Butter

 0
1 cup
Olive oil

 0
1 cup
Coconut oil

 1
Mayonnaise

 2
Tabasco / Hot sause

 3
Heavy cream

 3
Guacamole

 3
Vinaigrette

 4
Cream cheese

 4
Soy sause

 6*
Mustard

 6
Salsa

 8
Pesto

 15
Tomato paste

 26
Ketchup

 40
BBQ sause

 68
Maple syrup

 69
Jam

BEST ← CARBS → **WORST**

BERRIES AND FRUITS

Raspberry **5**

Blackberry **5**

Strawberry **6**

Coconut (Meat) **6**

Watermelon **7**

Cantaloupe **7**

Peach **8**

Orange **9**

Plum **10**

Cherries **10**

Clementine **10**

Blueberry **12**

Pear **12**

Kiwi **12**

Apple **12**

Pineapple **12**

Grapes **16**

Banana **20**

BEST ← **CARBS** → **WORST**

NUTS AND SEEDS

 0.6g
Pili nuts

 1.2g
Pecan

 1.4g
Brazil nuts

 1.5g
Macadamia

 2g
Hazelnut

 2g
Walnut

 2.6g
Almonds

 4g
Brazil

 5g
Pistachio

 7.7g
Cashews

 8g
Peanut

 0.4g
Flax seeds

 1.3g
Pumpkin seeds

 1.4g
Chia seeds

 2.7g
Pine seeds

 3.2g
Sunflower seeds

 3.3g
Sesame seeds

| BEST | ← CARBS → | WORST |

With the use of this ketoveo shopping list you can put together some yummy ideas of what you would like to eat for your future meal planning. Remember high fat, moderate protein & low carbs.

The goal of being on the keto diet is to get your body into a state of ketosis, which means your body is producing ketones (small fuel molecules) from burning fat and not from burning sugar and carbs to create energy for your body.

Ketones are produced when you are eating minimum carbs and moderate protein. This then takes the fats you eat and converts it into ketones by your liver that enter the blood stream. These ketones are then used as fuel by the cells in the body. They even happily fuel your brain! People feel more energized and focused when the brain runs on ketones, made from fat. This certainly speeds up fat loss being on a ketogenic diet with your body running on your fat as energy!

Following the Ketoveo plan can help you on your journey and lifestyle to getting your body healthy, energized and losing weight by getting your body into ketosis. We from Ketoveo welcome you to the tribe and look forward to your successful keto journey ahead.

Made in the USA
Middletown, DE
28 February 2020